Lucky Enough: A Journey

Lucky Enough: A Journey

poems
Nancy Kerrigan

GRAYSON BOOKS
West Hartford, CT
www.GraysonBooks.com

Lucky Enough: A Journey
copyright © 2019 Nancy Kerrigan
published by Grayson Books
West Hartford, Connecticut

Library of Congress Control Number: 2019915963

ISBN: 978-1-7335567-6-7

Book design by Cindy Stewart
Cover photo by Nancy Kerrigan, taken in Connemara County, Ireland
Author photo by Bill Crofton

In memory of James and Annamae Kerrigan

*In the city of Chicago
when the evening shadows fall
there are people dreaming
of the hills of Donegal.*

Christy Moore

Contents

Royalty
Leaving Home, Age Six	13
In the Cards	16
Ode to the Rainbow Cone	17
Lollygagger of the First Waters	19
Street Walkers	20
A Grandfather Imagined	21
Ironing It Out	22
My Grandmother's Wisdom	23
St. Patrick's Day	25
Christmas Eves	27
The Godfather	29
Royalty	30
For the Women Who Ride Buses	31
A Slice of Sisterhood	32
The Daily Donnybrook	33
An Open Wound	35
Mother Said	36

A Future in Past Tense
The Night the Mannequins Moved	41
How It All Began	42
Rude Awakening	43
If Only	44
The Fight	45
Your Own Viet Nam	46
Denouement	48
He Let Her Go	49
Two Women	50
A Future in the Past Tense	51
The Heart-Shaped Space	52
Mama Drama	53
Dancing at Lughnasa	54
A Fatherhood Observed	55
After	57
Estrangement	58

Hope
Hope Is	63
The Purple Metallic Convertible	64
Eastern Adulterer	66

Hartford, Connecticut	67
Doors	68
The Rocker	69
Men Working	70
Billy Collins Goes to Nantucket	72
The Mack House	74
I'm Watching the Television Show of My Life	75

Something About the Irish

Conversations on Clare Island	79
The Kerrigans Carry On	81
Kate, from County Sligo	82
Love Famine	83
Lucky Enough, Chicago 1960	84
Mothers in Mourning	86
A Celtic Lament	87
Irish Summers	88
Mo Cuishle: My Darling My Own	89

Seismic Shifts

Sonnet During a Storm	93
Getting Serious	94
Winter Solstice	95
Bocelli & You	96
White Space	97
Seismic Shifts	98
I Had a Dream	99
Homesick	100
Women's March on Washington	101

At Last This

The Field's Clock	105
Hand-Me-Downs	106
Santa Gets It Right	107
Playground Dust-Up	108
At Last This	109
Wellspring	110
Aurora	111
Harvested	112
Notes on the Poems	113
About the Author	114
Acknowledgments	115

Royalty

Leaving Home, Age Six
Evergreen Park, 1950

    I.

I see the commotion gathering.
Sooty screen imprints
tattooed on my forehead.
Curiosity & I push the screen
out my bedroom window.
It floats end over end, down
two stories in slow motion.
Men in white clothes lift Dad
on a stretcher into an ambulance.
Sheets, once white, wrapped on him
now have blood spots.
Faces look up. I duck.

Uncle John arrives.
He shoves our clothes & toys in pillow cases.
My brother and I trail behind.
Mother cradles our baby sister,
who screams for us all.
    You'll stay with Aunt Connie
    and Uncle John until school's out.
Aunt Connie opens their door
and never closes it again.
Our family nurse now cares for five
children under age six, two in cribs.
Next morning, Michael, age three,
sits Buddha like, crying
in front of a pile of his clothes.
I put his shoes on the right feet
so he can go out to play.

    II.

Mom leaves to walk back
to the shell of our house, empty
of everything but germs,

to work inside and outside our home.
No dish drying for me anymore;
dishes must be boiled.
No more coloring with Mom in my ballet book
pages uncolored to this day.
I ask, *What's T.B.?*
An army of grownups, soldiers every
last one of them, does not answer,
or I can not hear it.

Summer, still no Dad.
A new aunt & uncle, far away.
My girl cousins, a bit older
play long songs on their piano.
Uncle Matt calls me *Irish*.
   Isn't everybody?
   Not here.
Cousin Midge lets me try
to walk in her pink toe shoes.
Together we sleep in a big bed
in her own room. No one
slept alone at my home.
Aunt Marie sews us matching sun dresses;
drives us to a big amusement park.
I only go on one ride.
Mom never drove our Chevy.
Aunt Marie, a Cubs fan
takes us to Wrigley Field.
I like screaming there.
Janet, my oldest cousin
dreams up a playhouse
where we'll all live.
A rug makes a bedroom under
the ping-pong table, a kitchen
out of wooden crates.
Lampshades on liquor bottles,
curtains hung down for windows.

III.

Three months pass
like a wait for Christmas.
I am going home to go to school.
Nuns at our school wear white.
I promise to clean the house
on the drive back to the south side.
When I walk through the front door
my brother calls me: *Cousin Nancy*.
We rarely play together after
that summer away on Chicago's
north side when I became a Cubs fan.

In The Cards
Evergreen Park, 1954

Everyone played canasta,
at least on my block,
where half the neighbors were my relatives.
Swimming pools closed,
amusement parks closed.
Drinking fountains stood lonely
even the birds didn't splash.
There was nothing to do, nothing to do
but play canasta.
Canasta on the screened porch, in the living room
on a white sheet fresh
off the backyard clothes line.
We cousins cheated
like used car salesmen.
Afternoons were for rest,
so we children were not stricken
with that year's dread: polio.

For all we knew, the epidemic began
and ended in Evergreen Park.
The suburbs spread like some architectural disease.
Tree-lined streets of Georgians and Capes
encircled by new construction where we played.
Parents told us, a five-year-old girl on our block
had a lung of iron to help her breathe.
Why would her mother iron her lungs to help her breathe?
That fall, nurses lined us up like the books in the school library.
Shots, we were packed in that hot box waiting for shots.
A nun in a white habit with very long rosary beads
stood on the library's threshold to lasso bolters.
Titles on the books became a blur on my way down to the floor.
Total collapse, no. Stricken, no, just a faint.
Polio just a faint memory for the lucky.
I was lucky.

Ode to the Rainbow Cone

9233 South Western Avenue
Beverly Hills, Chicago

Fifty cents each, when Dad piles
three generations into the '53 Chevy.
Rainbow, the destination no one refuses.
I'd trade my only child to have one now.

Five colorful layers of ice cream wedges piled
atop one pointy sugar cone. If one fell off,
the three-minute rule applied. It's the orange sherbet
that first soaks onto the tongue, slightly tart, cool,

giving goose bumps on hot evenings. As adults we bike
to the parlor, run by one family, at one location, for 85
summers. We inhale one, guilt free. To hell with calories.
Cravings begin when the magnolias bloom.

The green pistachio layer, riddled with crunchy nuts,
drives me wild. How can you stand to feel this gourmand,
tickle around your odd shape? You cylinder of pleasure,
a confection that unites man, woman and child.

A scoop of *Palmer House Venetian Vanilla* follows,
filled with large, red maraschino cherries, stop lights
as I race down, licking each. This layer's trademark,
makes the cone Chicago's own, precludes imitation.

Now comes a full wedge of strawberry ice cream, seducing
the tongue. Frozen berries shock the mouth with their iciness.
I bite them even as they send little charges through my teeth.

Deep in the bowl of the sugar cone lives the rich dark chocolate,
the foundation for this ice cream sculpture. Dessert of all desserts,
you've been the appetizer, vegetable, and entree of many meals.

Like most journeys, it's better to have traveled than to arrive.
The last lick punctuated with oohs & ahs. A newcomer at the end
of the line shouts to the clerk in a white apron and envelope cap,
I'll have whatever she had!

Lollygagger of the First Waters

Good morning Glory,
your voice my alarm at the foot of the stairs.
Out of the bed, onto the stairway balcony
Lying, *I'm up Dad.*
Back in bed like a cuckoo clock.
I want to see you!
Smell of bacon and hot oatmeal my morning kiss.
I'd sit there, bare feet swinging
while I read the back side of your newspaper.
Lollygagging in flannel pajamas, pattering
around searching for favorite socks,
last night's homework,
anything to make the morning last.

Good morning Glory,
I say whacking the snooze bar
on my fifth Sony Dream Machine.
No game of hide and seek.
The instant coffee never fast enough,
downed with headlines unfit to print.
Dad, you're still the steam in my coffee,
a vapor that hangs around in my sphere,
gone for more sunrises than I can count.
Lollygagging lives on as I roam the sunlit house
watering plants, searching for misplaced keys.

Most mornings you enjoyed the impossible in me.
What more could I have asked of him?

Street Walkers

Nuns traveled in pairs,
a covalent bond
with positive and
negative powers.
Ever present, at the right
or wrong time, depending
on your perspective.
Some swaddled in layers
of heavy white muslin,
heads crowned with a long,
black, heart-shaped veil.
Did they have hair or
were they bald under there?

Dad often offered
to give a lift to these
spiritual streetwalkers
who made us memorize
the *Baltimore Catechism*.
A black & white text
with answers for
the unknowable.

Worried, I went to Dad.
Sister said, God calls you...
taps you on the shoulder.
At twelve I didn't want
to be called by anyone
not in my grade, didn't
want to be a habit,
even a good habit.

Jesus, Dad grumbled.
Then, in one sentence
Dad saved me, replying
God knows, Nancy,
you could not wear
the same thing every day.

A Grandfather Imagined

John J. Burns May 1, 1879, at rest August 25, 1939

Anna My Dear,

Living with my brother Charlie and his wife Mary since I came over tries my patience, now thin as paper. Sure he's a story a minute, but they will listen to my rhyming poetry. Two Chicago papers come out a day. I hide behind one in between routes. I read a poet named Edgar Guest. The *Tribune* publishes him. He's called *The Peoples Poet*. I try my hand at it, writing helps me stay. I mailed a letter to President Roosevelt to thank him for his fine speeches.

Sure I am driving motor buses all over the city. A man driving street cars on rails has to be punctual, steady, ye know that I'm that. Save us, getting round on foot was good enough on Clare Island, but not in this hectic town. There's talk of organizing, pensions. Unions here work for us. I joined, hope I live to collect one.

With your Mother passing, ye are now free to do the crossing. The big O'Malley clan can do without ye. Steerage is a penance like none other. Sometimes a sickness comes over ye, or is it sorrow pouring out of us for all we've waved goodbye to? I wish I could spare you this voyage over the ocean that has become a salty bowl, filled to the brim with all of our tears. You can rattle your rosary beads through your fingers for the entire passage. If you come, you can stay with my sister Nora. She'll help you find work serving the Protestants. They don't hate Catholics here as much as the English do. They teach housemaids how to do things proper. I'm tired of meself. Bring some of the old sod with ye, make me laugh with the quickness of your tongue.

With grand affection,

John

Ironing It Out

My grandmother taught me to iron.
I'd see her sprinkle our white uniform
blouses and long-sleeved shirts with water.
She'd roll the damp tops into a towel placing
them into the fridge to prepare for her next
day's work. A flick of water sizzle tested
the iron's readiness:

Start with the collar turned on its backside.
Stretch the button-less edge taut, slide the iron
over the unoccupied holes. Move to the other side.
Weave the nose of the iron round the plastic buttons.
Flip the shirt or blouse on its back to get to the
shoulders, then onto the sleeves, both of them...

Gram wore wrinkled, patterned housedresses.
Her thinning white hair rolled into a bun,
bobby pinned at her neckline, face flushed
by the time we came home from school.
We never even thought to thank her.

Perma-press, now is applied to fabrics. Magically
smoothing out wrinkles and moods, leaving us more
time to work harder somewhere else. Gram said:
We clean up nicely; appear as if we hadn't a care
in this messy world. To relax, I still enjoy starting out
for an evening on the arm of a man in a crisp, clean
dress shirt. Ending, his tie draped over the rear view
mirror, shirt sleeves rolled up, both of us rumpled.

My Grandmother's Wisdom
Anna O'Malley Burns 10-31-1873, at rest 3-20-1965

If too many possessions or gadgets appeared in the house:
   No wonder the potatoes would rot.
If she snitched on us, when we were really mean or lied:
   They were not beyond the praises of three
If Mom, the prosecutor found a suitable punishment:
   They'll have to dance according to the music.
If we were hungry, begging for dinner, Gram's retort:
   I can't go between it & the fire.
If found to be the cause of a donnybrook:
   Sure you'd force Christ to come down off the cross.
If I spent too much time primping at the mirror:
   Vanity of vanity and all is vanity.
If then she approved of my dates:
   He skinned out nicely or sure he's a long drink of water.
If social visits were infrequent:
   Who showed you the house?
If compliments were expected, but unearned:
   Your fame is further than your foot.
If recognition was earned, but unacknowledged:
   They are damned by faint praise.
If an offspring of a family member showed a trait like a relative:
   They didn't get that from the wind nor the weather.
If she felt particularly neglected:
   I am the last decade on your rosary beads.

She loved the in-laws like her own:
   As God made them, He matched them
She'd go out to mow the lawn herself if Dad & her son
sat glued to sports on TV:
   You two are so lazy, if you died you wouldn't stiffen.
She opened her home to Ireland's greenhorns, dismissed
their rare ungratefulness:
   Eaten bread is soon forgotten.
She wished them good luck when they found work and moved on:
   May you never be a day sick, sore or sorry.

Gram said often,
   If you are born to hang, you won't drown
but she did neither. Lived till ninety-two.

St. Patrick's Day

Chicago's river dyed green.
Mother, in our green lacquered kitchen
sits typing at the Royal, fingers
pounding, pounding,
step dancing on the keys.
Uncle John pacing like a beat cop,
awaiting each page as Mom
edits his television script.
Gram of the O'Malley clan,
shuffling between her children,
rosary beads in hand, holding off
another *Easter Rebellion*.

Parents as insistent as whistling tea kettles
I'm to compete for the Parade Queen.
But I'm a snotty sixteen.
Disdainful of everything Irish, ignorant
of famine, oppression, freedom wars
that left scars. What do I know of ancestors
fleeing across a sea with waves like mountains?

I do as I am told.
Gawked at by old men,
sashaying around in a green dress
with a number on my back,
I win a place in the Queen's court.
Queen Kolb crowned.
Uncle John grumbles:
Not a drop of Irish in her.
Dad whistles *The Rose of Tralee...*
t' was not just her beauty
that won her for me...

I sit erect with my hand cupped
rotating on a paper float
wearing a borrowed fur coat
that covers my goose flesh.

My blood from then on runs green,
I've had my first lesson
in doing a thing for the greater good
for dramatic folk who loved poetry,
and a chance to dance with stiff arms
and tapping feet.

Christmas Eves

After working full-time,
after shopping at Marshall Fields,
Mother made sure everyone had a gift,
even those who came
with one hand as long at the other.
Along with the faithful women
of her generation, Mom, Aunt Connie
and Anna May fed all the required meatless meal.

The collective Irish tempers
along with the electrical power sources
drained by Christmas lights, coffee makers,
and deep fryers led to the annual
Fuse Blowing Ceremony.
Darkness arrived, an uninvited guest.
Everything and everyone stopped.
For a few moments it was as if
a bookmark had been placed in a page
of the party. The night became sacred
in stillness and darkness.
Dad slipped secretly down to the basement
and magically relit the house.

When Mom shouted, *Kids, keep the tags!*
presents and thank-you notes were to follow.
Uncle John, born on the feast day of St. Nicholas,
took this serendipity to heart. Generous
365 days a year, his belly bloomed
each Christmas Eve, circled by the big belt
of Santa Claus. Calling each child by name,
he passed out presents. His son John II,
an eight-year-old sleuth, screamed his best
caught-ya. *Santa, you stole my Daddy's watch!*
Santa didn't miss a jingle: *Had to be on time!*

One Christmas Santa rode my 26-inch blue
Schwinn bike through our front door,
across the tiny vestibule, weaving between

kids on the floor. Our spruce tree wobbled.
Its silver tinsel rained down our blessings.
Our hearts were forever stolen.

The Godfather
John C. Burns, 12-6-1918, at rest 7-24-2003

As a child he must have dawdled
at the candy counter, jiggling pennies
in the pockets of his short pants.
Smelling the confections, promising
himself someday he'd be rich enough
to fill a closet full of the sweets.
He kept his word.

Candy circus peanuts, caramel cream Bulls Eyes,
Twizzlers, Jujubes, Chuckles,
popping the tops off of their glass jars
lined up on shelves in his family room.
Double door closet open 24 hours a day—
and free. Drooling began when your sneakers
crossed the threshold. Fire balls, jaw breakers,
bubble gum cigars and cigarettes.
Uncle John, a dentist's worst nightmare,
never believed a dinner could be spoiled.
These were just appetizers for kids.

On stage, on screen, an actor who knew
his part in front of and behind the camera.
We lined the local theater rows, listened to him
on the radio, encircled the T.V. His mother
didn't live to see him don the red cap and black robes
of a Cardinal in the play *The Cardinal's Two Hats*
in downtown Chicago. His older sister simply noted
their Mother would have thought him saintly.

He moved in aging relatives, delivered them
to his caring wife, our nurse. To miss a wake or
funeral of a neighbor or friend, his notion of mortal sin.
On occasion, he arrived at the wrong parlor, stayed on
anyway to pay his respects to the unknown corpse:
The poor bastard had no one saying a prayer.

Royalty

Princess Diana's dresses under Plexiglas.
I stroll this exhibition with solemn school girls
in jeans and sneakers, who stare at the sequined splendor,
then gaze at blue-jean mommies.
Each reads about the galas where these gowns
made an entrance to dance,
outliving the royal who gave them
scent, swing and rustle.
No music, soft lights, whispering one, two, left, right.
We knew everything and nothing of this woman's life.

I lament Diana had no daughters—you have two.

You held court in the powder room.
With my braids done and jumper on, I focused
my freckled face on you curling your eyelashes,
straightening your seams
before you slipped on your platform high heels.
Your face mysterious behind the veil of your hat,
the final curtain before we left for the ballet.
You, in a soft fur coat.
Your perfume filled the small space like incense.

Now, your scent eludes me. I search perfumeries—discontinued.

You are on the magazine covers in my mind,
as beautiful as any goddess, beautiful as Diana.
Not a commonplace mother,
the pages of your life, no fairy tale. My love,
there is no place to wear a wide brimmed hat and white gloves.
We dress for a dance where pants would do,
high heels instead of sensible shoes.
Dressed for a life we did not lead.
If we were not royalty, we never knew.
Our femininity fashioned by you.

For the Women Who Ride Buses

Rosa, since 1955 you've sat, and sat, and sat
in our minds on that Montgomery city bus

would not give up your seat to a white man.
You weren't the first black woman who refused

to go to the back of the bus, but you are the one
etched in the black and white of our memory.

You sat there dignified in your cloth coat
with your hat on, staring out of that bus window.

Were you planning dinner under that hat,
plotting to change history, or just plain tired?

How many bus rides did it take to make you see the,
steam rising up through your straw pill box,

before you decided not to move? Your own name
not among the P's in my 1980 encyclopedia.

In that decade of *Father Knows Best*, my mother worked
outside the home too, wearing a hat much like yours.

Often, she neglected to take it off while she cooked dinner.
Mornings, she ran in high heels to catch her two buses,

consumed one library book after the next, the commute so long.
Some days rain washed away her makeup, or was it rain?

Thanks to the women who traveled unfamiliar routes before me,
I drive to my own office where I listen to the plight of women

not behind the wheels of their lives, waiting in the rain
for buses to take them to the night shift at Wal-Mart.

A Slice of Sisterhood

Your former fiancé bought himself
a *Rolex*, leaving your ring finger
naked as a plucked daisy.
You broke the engagement.
We spot him with another woman.
So debonair, he presents himself,
grazes your cheek with a kiss. Your
bright smile, no indication you cared.
It had been awhile. The next morning
my shoulder yours.

Once at six you cried like this.
You jumped on the back fender
of my big blue Schwinn bike as if
it were the family station wagon.
With one bike and six years between us,
we were off to buy school supplies
a mile away. Buicks and Chevies
whizzed by us. Your scream
let me know your ankle
had been sliced open by the spokes.
A cameo scar remains.

Didn't *Aftershave*, your fiancé, know
you were the Princess of Kindergarten?
I dressed you in patent pumps & party dresses.
Your blond hair styled each afternoon;
one day a pony tail, another a bow. You
were the prettiest baby doll I ever had.
Until my fun was spoiled by the nun
who told Mother kindergarten was not
a birthday party. We knew it was.
Jo, every doll has a name. Those that love
you know, all scars are not visible.

The Daily Donnybrook

Dad tossed keys
to a used 1960 black
Beetle towards me.
Never found reverse
on my maiden drive.
The VW purchased
on the condition that
my brother & I would
share it on campus.
He was asking two
college kids to share
a five pack of beer.

I need it for my date!
I want to go downtown.
Give me the keys!
I won't let you in.
$3 filled the gas tank.
Yet after his date,
the gauge read empty.

On snow-packed streets
the button-sized tires fell
into Buick-sized tracks.
360-degree spin outs
demonstrated the car's
perfect center of gravity.
Your right foot, the one
body part that warmed.
The gas pedal fell off
on the expressway
when put to the metal.
No seat belts made it
a near death experience.

The bug still takes me places.
If Dad could see us now,
fights fizzled out.
Arguments today about
who gets an A in Religion.
In our respective corners, there's
a Catholic in fourth gear in one,
a casual Catholic in neutral in the other,
but we both still have faith.

An Open Wound

Each generation has a disease to dread.
Galloping consumption was a name for Dad's lung disease.
From the age of six I heard coughing in our home.
Dad worked when he could; Mom worked when he couldn't.

Galloping consumption was a name for Dad's lung disease.
An open fist sized wound on his back kept draining.
Dad worked when he could; Mom worked when he couldn't.
We all learned to change the dressing on his back.

An open fist sized wound on his back kept draining.
Dad lay down to have it changed. Mom made faces he never saw.
We all learned to change the dressing on his back.
Bakery éclairs for dessert when he sold the insurance he couldn't get.

Dad lay down to have it changed. Mom made faces he never saw.
My goal, to be a nurse, get smart and make him feel better.
Bakery éclairs for dessert when he sold the insurance he couldn't get.
My brother went to the links to change Dad's dressing after golf.

My goal, to be a nurse, get smart and make him feel better.
Outwardly this was as normal for us as slipping on clean socks.
My brother went to the links to change Dad's dressing after golf.
When other men looked on, this was something they never forgot.

Outwardly this was as normal for us as slipping on clean socks.
When other men looked on, this was something they'd never forget.
He left three college graduates without a penny in student debt.
A gift he gave freely, but one he never got.

Mother Said

*You must have something to think about while
you peel potatoes over the sink.*

Mom never denied domestic chores awaited me.
Grocery shopping, meal planning, and ironing loomed
like a marathon for which I hadn't trained.
Mashing potatoes required biceps; she did this
without a mix-master. Among her well-earned truths

*If you can read, you can cook,
and Knowledge is the only thing worth vacuuming up.*

Daughter of the Great Depression and Irish immigrants.
Admitted to Rosary College, but she could not matriculate.
She settled for business school instead of teaching.
Insisted I write; no typing courses for me.

*Take more French, don't take a job
where you need to hunch over a machine.*

I enrolled at Loyola University to live in a dormitory
with closets the size of a phone booth. No jeans or slacks
permitted on female students on campus. Complaining
to Mom about the lack of a wardrobe, she proclaimed

We sent you here to fill your head, not your closet.
My retort: *There is no reason I can't do both.*

Mother, hunched over her Royal to type my Master's thesis.

Get your nose out of those psychology books, she told me,
read some literature to learn how real people behave.

Mom made us love to read, if only to avoid chores.
After she died my sister & I hauled hundreds of her novels
and political books to the local library in Chicago's
105-degree heat, our last summer together there.

Though a reader, I haven't yet mastered the fine art of cooking.

A Future in the Past Tense

The Night the Mannequins Moved

No one was in the furniture store, no one.
Doors locked. No escape.
Fiancé heard the mattresses calling to him.

Nan imagined the morning headlines:
Burglars Found Sleeping on the Job.
His '65 Mustang in full view across the street.

He collapsed on a couch. Outside, a slight,
unshaven man toting a small brown paper sack
glanced twice, then staggered down the street.

In panic, Nan pounded the plate glass window.
In time blue squad lights illuminated the avenue.
With hands flat on the glass, they were fish in a dry bowl.

The owner, bath robe flapping, rattled his keys on arrival.
The men in blue serge grumbled that an old drunk prattled on
about mannequins moving on Western Avenue.

Later, making out on their new couch, they recalled the owner
did not check his register drawer. Fiancé imitated the cop
Hands off her, buddy...we were all young once.

Nan loved his forward moves, his go-with-the-flow attitude.
She just didn't want to cook dinner for the rest of her life,
disliked being locked in, couldn't let others design
a pattern for her future. She feared an upholstered life.

How It All Began

Charles, her knight with character for armor.
To love & cherish the memorable ever-more.
Both were ready to close other doors.

Charles. her knight with character for armor.
No need for forgetting, they had not done this before.
Could they live out the memorable ever-mores?

Walking down the aisle who knows how it ends?
Nan knew life would be smoother dancing with him.
Wedding vows so easy to speak, yet hard to amend.

Walking down the aisle who knows how it ends.
Over the years they'd become great friends.
Bridesmaids and groomsmen sang on a whim.

Walking down the aisle who knows how it ends.
Wedding vows promised before family and friends.
One young couple left singing, ready to begin.

Rude Awakening

A high school marching band
practiced under the third floor
bedroom window of the life guard
and the almost beauty queen.
Every married morning
they awakened to music.
Anthems and Sousa marches.
Suddenly the music turned
ominous.
The drum section
pounded and pounded, no
other instruments heard;
the cymbals, smashed together
repeatedly throughout the piece.
Headaches would not abate.
He was late.
She was late.
They had fallen into troubled waters.
Both thrashed in Lake Michigan's
black depths.
He, the better swimmer,
was going under. She
just screamed for help.
The life preservers had faces.
Rescuers kept their heads above water.
Total strangers pulled them to shore.
For the first time in their marriage
they slept separately.
Hospital beds not made for two.
Her crown, made of paper.
Sometimes all you have is a year
to prepare for a storm.

If Only

His long arms encircled her six-month belly from behind.
Standing, her back leaned into him. The baby kicking Dad's
folded hands to get out for all the world to see. But no one
could get out in Chicago's blizzard of '67. On the bed snow drifts

of her dresses, skirts, slacks she couldn't get into; he couldn't zip.
Together they shopped maternity stores, jostling on elevated trains
the one mode of transport that moved. Whiteouts blind you
to what's ahead, but keep you centered on what's important.

Like avoiding Nam, writing your Master's thesis. This longed for
event that linked them to & for life, began in their honeymoon year.
It could have been savored, sipped solemnly like a sacred wine
if only they knew then, it would never come again.

The Fight

His golf clubs were her wedding gift to him.
At Notre Dame he played eighteen to escape studies.
After surgery he felt happy to be alive and working;
she was happy for a summer off. Golf the one sport
he believed he could play post-op. Not a Country Club Couple,
this work-related event brought them to one.
Tanned, showered, he slung his seer sucker sport coat
over a shoulder, but looked so serious. She hooked onto his arm
as they entered the Watering Hole bar before dinner.

She looked too fancy in a floor length beige linen skirt,
three-inch high heels peeking out from under her dress.
Elegant, no flesh exposed as she entered the club bar.
One gray haired man after another, in golf shirts and shorts,
half on and half off bar stools, pulled her toward them,
kissed her flushed cheek, touched her cold shoulders.
Smiling because she usually did, thought she should.
The more they grabbed her, the further back she tipped,
She was the only woman in the bar. None of the other
men brought wives. They shook his hand too, pulling him
away from her. Glancing over her shoulder her look said:
I am leaving. I don't belong here.
He stayed.

Driving home alone, she remembered
how she fell asleep on his shoulder on the plane flight
to their San Francisco honeymoon; she felt so loved
when he told anyone who would listen that she was his wife.
Thoughts came roaring back, recalling their fun dancing,
the cold Saturdays cheering on the Fighting Irish.
Her thoughts so loud she heard them herself:
He didn't know; he wouldn't do this.

It took her years to figure out where she belonged.
That was the last time he tried to play golf.
Brain surgery slowly robbed him of memory, balance,
coordination. From blocks away that day, she could hear
the Catholic church bells ring the Angelus.

Your Own Viet Nam

You said you had
your own Viet Nam
though you never touched a gun.
Not drafted—you had no choice.
Brain cut open twice, misfired like
mortar rounds, commanding you
to fall down, bite your tongue.
Pain overcame words.
Headaches forced a high pitched
cry, like an animal about to expire.
You survived. We danced around in circles.
You fought on the home-front.

Quietly, lights darkened
in the rooms of your brain, as if
we had not paid the bills.
Legs weakened. Shrapnel? No.
A proliferation of cells. Hearing
dimmed, only one ear wired.
Far-sighted, but no side vision.
Speech came in slow motion.
Gait tipsy, but not a drop to drink.

Recent memory faded,
a television pilot seen once,
not renewed, but good times
from the past—in living color.
Unable to walk, you became
a prisoner of this war,
couldn't go out on your own,
wheelchair-bound.

The unseen enemy, never whined
about, rarely mentioned.
With these words, I salute you.
You spent more than half of your life
defending the very privilege of having one.
No promotion in rank. No Purple Heart.
No honor after war like its veterans.
Even the strongest soldiers fall.

Denouement

Can't remember the last time I held our daughter's hand
crossing the street, or the last time I brushed her hair.
But I'm aware that lifting my granddaughters
is coming to an unwanted close.

Can't recollect the time I could read without glasses.
So many of life's important endings slip by unnoticed,
ice cubes melting on the counter.

I can clearly recall a summer evening with no moon
but you, lying on backyard grass with every star
ours for the taking, the naming, entering the heavens.

Abundance and possibility wrapped around us
like a zippered sleeping bag. Years passed.
Our denouement, equally etched in my mind.

Me, with my forehead on your chest, your chin on my head,
as we stood arms at our sides, facing one another, facing,
accepting what we both knew to be inevitable. We would
not reach the end together; our stars were not aligned.

He Let Her Go

On the day they met with his attorney from Notre Dame
On the day alimony was demanded from her by his lawyer

On the day he rose on two legs, his cane falling to the floor
On the day he shouted to his lawyer, *Leave her alone*

On the day she sat, head lowered, heard how he loved her
On the day they both agreed to do what must be done

On the day he gave her a bouquet of white calla lilies
On this day with these three words he let her go and held her.

Two Women

Bullets blasted his brains
all over your pink suited life.
Black veiled Madonna,
two young children at your side,
while a country tried to console you.
All he worked for and symbolized you inherit.
His flaws covered the way fresh fallen snow
covers up an old, established neighborhood.

My love's brain destroyed from the inside.
Alone as I chose, I exited the court house.
My hands wringing his handkerchief.
Our weaknesses written into public decree.
Doubt my legacy, guilt my companion,
annulment my church's absurd answer.
A rupture in the genealogy,
our daughter, the families' pawn.

The men are gone.

A Future in the Past Tense

an artist's framed
pencil sketch
a house of dreams
a flagstone chimney
cirrus clouds above
a front lawn
with grass and hedges
that never need cutting
a scene so easily erased
save for this artist's
rendering

a young mother
a little girl
look out of a large
picture window
peep from behind
pleated white drapes
forever waiting
for a young husband
to pull up the long drive
in his Mustang, vintage '65

a first chapter cut short
a wound unhealed
a book never finished
a threshold no second child
ever crossed

The Heart-Shaped Space

It was finally off
the front page of her life.
Nan paid her bills on time,
managed to mow the lawn
before the dog got lost in it.
She'd begun dating someone
who almost made her forget, but
like some chronic infection

a divorce fever broke out
each year around Christmas.
Temperatures elevated, some
complained of lumps in their throats.
Now they are called a broken family.

This year was an odd year. It wasn't
her turn to have the holiday.
She sat in their old bedroom,
brooding, beholding the first snowfall
clothing the naked cherry tree
with limbs once divided by
the presence of electrical wires.
A nearly heart shaped space
remained after the tree survived
the heat and force of the wires.

The tree outside their window
nonetheless, bloomed every
spring, holding empty a place
for what was.

Mama Drama

Act I.

Criminal torture, my daughter griped about the sound coming from her bathroom toilet. I bent the arm of the floating ball in the tank, as directed in my *New York Times Guide To Home Repair*, a divorce gift. A geyser zoomed upward, the tank lid rose three feet. Water squirted into her bedroom and soaked my sweats. My sneakers squeaked as I went to greet Joe, the plumber & his son. It was a holiday. Appliances keep track of holidays. As Joe & I searched the house for the shut off valve, his son negotiated a prom date with my daughter. *Do it again, Mom!*

Act II.

This time flooring issues drove me to my knees. By now my high school senior & I were working together like two students climbing the same staircase. Large strips of carpet, shoved with our shoulders in the direction of her bedroom door. We lodged a six-foot ball of the wall-to-wall wool in her doorway, not an easy task. Neither of us were ever exiting the room until I light-bulbed the idea of gently lowering her out her bedroom window. Don't call the authorities yet, it was a ranch house. *Go get Painless*, our next-door dentist. *He's good at extractions. Mom, someday I'll walk a Red carpet.*

Act III

It was a smooth transition from *Play-Doh* to cookie dough. Baking together became our Christmas tradition. Never again would I substitute *crème d' menthe* in the recipe for rum ball cookies. That year no one binged on them due to their green tinge. They remained in the cookie tin until March. These escapades come back to me the way my inside-out umbrella did that Christmas, when I let the wind take it where it would. A Good Samaritan returned it. It all comes back to me, her dreams, these one-act days, where for a brief moment in time she was all mine. My daughter and I unbroken in our broken world.

Dancing at Lughnasa
for Ellen & Rich

I am transfixed by you, my daughter
as the character Chris, the youngest of four
spinster sisters in this drama about Irish women
in the 1930s. You transport me and your Chicago
family to Ballybeg, County Donegal, Ireland
with a brogue so crisp, dancing so spontaneous
we are convinced you were born over there.

In Act I the sisters break into separate, sensual
dance moves where love seems briefly possible.
Music bounds out of their 1936 wireless radio.
Pent up emotions about barely subsisting,
trapped by routine chores of feeding chickens,
hauling water slow the frenzy. Only the oldest
sister has a job and that is threatened.

Chris, the youngest sister, has a son, Michael,
born out of wedlock, who's the love child for all.
You play Chris, defiant in her shameless ongoing
love for the child's father, a dancer who waltzes
in and out Michael's and her life. With each visit
Mother & son fantasize on stage that he will stay.
Your dialogue, singing and dancing make me
forget you are my daughter.

The joy of seeing my daughter act
overpowered my sadness of her leaving to begin
a new life with her fiancé, who will take over my job,
replace me to become her partner and promoter.
Lughnasas' narrator, Michael, enthralled by his mother's
brief dose of joy also defied sadness. Memory
of these moments will sustain us while we carry on.

A Fatherhood, Observed

He could not carry her as a toddler.
His balance stolen from him, so he sat
on the floor, his long legs crisscrossed
to build blocks and have tea.

He could not carry her as a preschooler, except
when she joyfully leapt in front of his Mustang.
Scared, he carried her up a flight of stairs,
bumping into walls to drop her into bed.

He could not walk on the beach with his cane,
so he built sand castles. Taught her to float looking
up at him; dive into the waves that brought her
back to him. She became the lifeguard he once was.

He taught her and his middle school students
the science he studied at Notre Dame University.
Homework nights were his. He understood their
awkwardness and forgetfulness were not permanent.

He could not drive after awhile, but taught her
to meet her goal. Never cursed if she blew a stop sign.
But took her to a cemetery to practice where she
couldn't kill a living soul.

He could not dance with her, though he once led
without making me feel led. Instead he came to size
up a bunch of gangly guys who couldn't fill his shoes.
He said to her, *You make the dress look beautiful.*

He could not haul his daughter and her entire
bedroom away to college, so he rubbed the neck
of her exhausted mother from the passenger seat
who thanked him by planting kisses on his cheek.

He could not escort her down the aisle as a bride.
She, on the arm of his younger brother, her Godfather.
He in a tux, tucked in a wheel chair, parked, waiting
at the alter to kiss her good-bye.

After

If I stayed could I have loved you more?
Maybe we could have made it for awhile longer.
You needed me to care for you.

If I stayed I could have hated you.
You would need me, not love me.
Maybe we could have made it for awhile longer.

If I stayed could I have taken care of you?
I supported three of us, tried for awhile.
You could love, but could not provide for us.

If I stayed it would not be my life.
Would I have loved myself?
Who would have supported me?

Your people supported you.
I stayed put for five years without you, for her.
I was rarely mentioned or spoken to, except by you.

I did not stay, moved away to work, to pay.
Was rarely mentioned or spoken to, except by you.
We supported each other more, the further apart we got.

Until we could not.

Estrangement

For children and parents facing unwanted separations

Daughter, we both left home
You left for college. I left to work.
The stability of our lives
traded for relief, for promise.
I drive past Hartford's Union Station
imagine you might be standing there,
ear buds in, backpack
stuffed with dirty laundry.
Your trips to visit,
never long enough
to satisfy my lonely heart,
never short enough
for your cautious one.
Our partings did not soften,
rather cracked open
crusts of earlier wounds.

I left you alone in a crib not your own,
with no reason offered
as to why or where I was going
or when I would return.
I did not know.
Separations are housed
in a small closet in our brains
with no knob on the door.
Early memories stored there,
before you knew words to describe them.
My voice blubbered across telephone wires.
Adults held the receiver to your tiny ear.
Its sound produced cascades of tears.
These grownups asked I not call.
Lullabies sung by your Gram
tried to put you to sleep. You did not sleep.
No one mentioned you cried
for your Dad, who wasn't there.
Does it matter to a child whether a father
is in a hospital or gone to look for a job?

As you leave me again to marry,
I know from our first separation forward,
the door of your love for me
had a tight hinge never fully open
without squeaking, you
with no understanding why.

Hope

Hope Is

leaving all you love and hate,
driving from the Midwest
in a Japanese compact car
a sewing machine
for an engine,
buttons for wheels,
at midlife with all needed
possessions behind you,
family photos, a tennis racket,
favorite albums and tapes
across that run-on-sentence
of a state, Pennsylvania,
for a job the natives won't take;

witnessing a double rainbow,
colors exquisite in the gray
mountain fog, beeping
at unknown drivers to look
beyond their low beams,

me believing a new life awaits.

The Purple Metallic Convertible

was the last loaner on the lot
on a top down day in May.
With the family sedan safely
in the mechanic's hands, I peeled
away from the dealership.
Convertibles automatically subtract
ten years off your driver's license.
Midlife mother became *Lolita* in sunglasses
with blond hair flying in a car I'd never pick.
Driver's honked as my briefcase
Bounced to the Beach Boys:
*... fun, fun, fun 'til her Daddy
takes her T-Bird away...*
sometimes a day just takes you.

Sometimes a day just takes you,
like a one-hundred-dollar bill in the envelope day,
or a sudden call from a long-lost lover day,
that takes you to a secret room in yourself,
and you burst right through its closed door

in a purple metallic convertible
with the Beach Boys blarin'
and you do something you've never done
before, like blow off a work day,
or spend all the money on yourself,
or go out with the married man.

And even if it rained all day on the beach,
or the money only purchased useless lottery tickets,
or the long-lost lover was nothing more than an oil slick,
that night in the convertible
with your hair hung over the head rest,
while you gaze at the moonlit night,

you feel satisfied that you sampled
the cookies when they were passed,
that you searched around that room
you never explored.

Sometimes we just need to shift into another gear.

Eastern Adulterer

It's been years since we've lived together, Chicago.
You, the Second City, were my first love. My regular guy,
neck of your rented tuxedo shirt unbuttoned, tie loosened.
In your gilded ballrooms, like old movie sets, we danced 'til
dawn, sped down Lake Shore Drive, parked to see the sun rise.

Home of the Cubs, the Sox, the Bulls, and the Bears
where winners and losers, saints and sinners
are loved just the same. The Sandburgs, Carl and Ryne,
the Richard Daleys, and even Al Capone.
A city of riots, schemes and scandals, where a passerby
will look you straight in the eye

Your skyline, never receding, became more beautiful with age.
Skyscrapers that loom out of the lake were big brothers,
who towered over to protect me. City of big shoulders,
near which I laid my head each night, I left
your weathered, unshaven face, fearful that the passion
had drained from our forty-year marriage.

Soon Hartford's Brook's Brothers bureaucrats were breathing
down my neck, suitable men turned into Aetnoids by the other world
of insurance; actuarial tables more important than musical scales.
But any city with writers' houses in a row seemed a luxury
for any literary high brow. Your Sunken Garden wooed me
with warm words that gently kissed my cheeks.

Captivated by your quaint New England charm, awed by your
brainy schools and good looks, I've become a eastern adulterer,
sleeping here for awhile, savoring each fall, never awakening
in a bed that feels like my own, arising each morning with the
question, how can a nine to five town ever be home?

That's when I fly back to you, Chicago, but you cannot hold me
for long. Why don't I choose one of you, and finally settle down?

Hartford, Connecticut

In Chicago, thumbing through nursing journals
searching for a job, one in Hartford grabbed me.
A large private psychiatric hospital,
hundred-year-old buildings surrounded
by pink dogwoods and coral azaleas. Manicured
lawns and grounds, designed by Olmstead,
held a swimming pool and tennis courts.
Move me, if you want me, I said. And they did.

I knew no one and no one knew me.
Inside, stood *quiet* rooms that were rarely quiet.
I met patients so kind, so ill, so deluded, they
feared the foam furniture we sat on would absorb us.
I treated aging patients who didn't know their wives or children.
Worked with children, their parents, protecting some
from abusers, like the ones who punished their kids
by forcing them to kneel on rice. I worked with them
and they with me.

I knew no one and no one knew me.
In newsletters, I read about Connecticut's nurses.
Activists, self-employed mind menders, whom I wanted to know.
I found them, one pearl at a time, at meetings, at conferences,
conventions. On the move, willing to upset the status quo—
women like me with a string of degrees, who listened carefully.
This strand of pearls turned into jewels of friendships.

I worked with them and they with me.
We formed a Society, letter bombed insurance agencies
to get patients access to psychiatric nurses. Hired lobbyists,
presented testimony in the lion's den of the state legislature—
fought for the legal right to prescribe. Slowly this city,
with tree lined highways that looked like a vacation drive, became
a city where I could work, live, make a difference. Maybe stay.

Doors

Their door opens slightly, as you learn
what brings them to you. Make friends
with quiet and the politeness of beginnings.

Crossing & uncrossing your legs to get
comfortable, to change your perspective,
then invite them to change theirs.

In time, the story, the gush of pain,
each word, paddles that start, have
scarred or hardened the heart.

Rub your eyes, sift through your own
unspoken memoir, check yourself,
while the sand drifts down the hour glass.

Be the scrim for this drama, see many sides,
yet filter the sadness, part the fog, direct
the water deepening in such a small space.

Listen, connect notes, what you hear, don't,
what's off key. What refrain keeps coming
back, or do they need to change their tune?

Life is a woven cloth. Pull a thread, change
the pattern. When some threads unravel, you
stitch, you patch, reattach the severed parts.

The door clicks shut. You collapse in
your chair. Breathe, take a deep breath
wrap both your arms around yourself,

open your window to the real world.
See the sun, watch the snow, smell the rain
look over roof tops.

Next patient...

The Rocker

Tonight, as I exit my office,
my chair is still rocking.
Does your ghost occupy it after I leave?
My chair in which no one else sits.
My chair which comforts me
as I spend my day listening to others.
A teen asks, *do you sing lullabies?*

An unfinished rocker we bought together long ago.
Stain you brushed on then, now worn off its edges.
This, our first purchase meant for Mother & the child
we had not met yet. You became a father in it too.
It waltzed from the family room to my office
when I had a home office. Later it rocked
in rented offices in another state
as I practiced my profession.

Now I imagine you are here with me each day.
Its arms are your arms, holding me
as I face limits, my own and others.
Will it keep rocking until I retire?
I'd like to shrink it down to doll house size.
Have a friend place it on my grave, so the strong
breezes of the *Windy City* will keep it rocking,
since I won't be buried next to you.

Men Working

Hard hats stand among orange cones.
One with a hand on a stick, *slow down* written on it.
The other hand pats down the summer air.
Semis swoosh by. He leans into the downdraft,
turning like a weather vane.

Linemen perched on telephone poles, legs stretched out
like Baryshnikov. Their bare hands connect
wired circuitry complex as our nervous system.
I peek from behind the front blinds. They could ignite
a spark or two in me.

Those city guys that cross high rise girders, how do they
catch their breath to whistle? Of course it's only for me.
Arms open wide as they go heel to toe across the tightrope
of beams, hands steady. Onlookers face upward,
all eyes fixed, our lips moving in prayer.

The rescuers save us from ourselves. The cop's hand
crosses my open car window, brushing my cheek.
Our eyes lock. His hand grabs mine as I turn over my license:
Ma'am, do you know how fast you're going?
I hear: *how fast we're going.*

Knee surgeons, the carpenters of medicine—mine bends
on his patella to slip on my shoe, as I sit upright
above him on the examining table. I'm Cinderella
in silver sneakers. He becomes my prince in blue scrubs
who will help me to dance again.

But who's my Steady Eddy? The guy whose hands
kept my Japanese excuse for a car running
until my daughter earned her college degree.
The mechanic who picked me up one distress call
after another, always bringing along his tank of gas.

I'm feeling warm, downright hot. I hear sirens
and fall in love with firemen. I smell smoke.
They've come to put out my heart's flame. Their ladders
are high. I'm afraid of heights. I want to know the feeling
of being carried to safety. But how could I ever let go?

Billy Collins Goes to Nantucket

The Art of Drowning,
not hard to master
on Cisco beach
where shark tooth waves
have bitten off the asphalt road—
now *the road not taken*.

Housemates all suspended
on this teeter-totter of time
in children's college sweatshirts,
retirement beckoning like a fog horn.
As we bike against the limits of heart and lung,
blue hydrangeas, pink impatiens, and youth pass us by.

Beach and Billy for breakfast, lunch and dinner,
poems as hors d' oeuvres, as blessings.
Robert Frost lovers bear with me.
When I love, I love passionately.
Nothing more to decide than dinner,
wine glasses, sand chairs, and watermelon sunsets.

Billy Collins, where are you?
Behind walls men who don't belong to me are snoring
while you are down on the coffee table.
I am one *of the languorous girls who would pass
long, limp summer evenings reading
Cherry Ames student nurse, Cherry Ames Flight Nurse*
Nurse Nancy needs the likes of you to fall asleep,
to walk the beaches of Nantucket.

Floyd, the not so perfect storm bears down.
Town boarded up, we commit to stay.
Bottled water—preparation, instead of evacuation,
Rain comes, syllables of rain,
whipped into words, full sentences.
Wind, like life can push you around.

Walk backwards to the beach,
black of night, flickering flashlights
sand stinging our for cheeks.
After the storm, shore rearranged—
we sing, we sway, we are the waves, the ocean,
tempting the tempest, that's all. Smell of fall.

Back to the swamp of middle age,
complex as any cranberry bog on this island.
So fortunate to have had these days with you, Billy
and a taste of this croissant in the Atlantic
to sustain us through the seasons to come.

The Mack House
Nantucket, Massachusetts

I thought it was mine.
the way my four-year-old daughter
believed the book *The Lonely Doll* was hers.
Out of the library it came, each time
we biked over to get something to read,
child in the carrier seat. Other books
selected, but this Dare Wright book
rode home until I bought it for her.
Finding it in the same place trip after trip
turned out better than owning it.

I thought it was mine.
Four summer vacations
idled away at this rental home.
Five bedrooms filled with friends,
and friends of friends who became friends;
children and grandchildren running about
who became our children. Cisco beach
within walking distance, we were lulled to sleep
with crashing waves. An ocean of generosity
floated from room to room. The upper outside deck,
so elevated, we felt we kissed the stars,
understood the complexities of the universe.

I thought it was mine.
I've rented movies, a car, even a bed
and a small jazz combo. They never felt like mine.
I read *The Lonely Doll* to my granddaughters, hoping
I will grow out of this phase where we think
we possess all that we love.

I'm Watching the Television Show of My Life

Again. It's a renewing dramatic series.
I'm obsessed with the script.
Just an ordinary love story
that includes a train wreck.
Cars collide, go off the rails.
Blinded by the sun,
Some can't see what's to come.
Hospitals visited
all day long; all day long.
Live with it; live with it.
Patients can't get off this train.
I want to get off this train.
I want them to get off this train
with me. A child sings:
Hey Jude make it better; better, better.
Cooking smells. School bells.
I get off that train and onto another.
Operatic music plays in the background:
Con Te Part Tiro. Time To Say Goodbye.
A rusty, leaky faucet drips down
all day long; all day long.
Some others try to turn it off,
like parrots repeat:
It's not your fault; it's not your fault.
Back to the script, revise—
I can't say goodbye.
I can't get to a different ending.
Shame colors my name;
my eyes turn green.
Puddles of rusty water deepen.
I stand alone at a casket.
I hear a voice with
no one else in the parlor:
You did nothing wrong, nothing wrong.
Forgiveness comes to visit,
but won't stay long.
Please God,
change the channel.

Something About the Irish

Conversations on Clare Island

Are ye immigrating back? asks the sea captain, muscling
on my coffin-like suitcase. Half of one life preserver hangs
on this WWII vessel; dark thoughts of drowning emerge.

A crumbling castle rises into view. It once belonged
to Grace O'Malley, *Granuaile*, The Irish Pirate.
My grandparents sailed from this island over 100 years ago.

First door I knock on opens: *Are ye Annamae Kerrigan's
daughter? You're her image!* We're driven to meet John
O'Malley, son of Michael, Gram's deceased oldest brother.

I cross the threshold of the stucco O'Malley cottage she never
crossed again after she left. I hear her chant: *Grief behind me,
grief before, and the wide Atlantic from shore to shore.*

Jamesons offered, not coffee. I hum *Too Ra Loo Ra Loo Ral*.
John sings *Minstrel Boy*, a school ditty Gram sang to me,
together we sing *Galway Bay*. Words flow like the liquor.

Proud fighters, we O'Malleys, he adds, head down: *Your
grandmother sent me passage, but I couldn't condescend,*
Gram ended some arguments: *I always enjoy a good fight.*

He claims my great grandmother, Nancy Burns,
was *fit to sing 'til the day she died.* An enviable epitaph.
I may have been named for her, but can't sing a note.

*The Burns families are fierce smart and the greediest
bunch, you'd ever meet,* says John. *Wasn't Chicago's Burns
Construction Company, their family pride?* He agrees.

He escorts me outside in wellies. I straddle the fence where
Gram broke her leg. He recites her oft told story of his father,
Michael, the Island's veterinarian, setting it.

A mainland Bishop crossed Clew Bay for Michael to set his
broken arm. This Bishop's framed wall photo glares at me
all morning. We hike past the church, stroll to the cemetery.

Surnames are as known to me as the lines on my hands.
We climb to cliffs at the edge of the island: *Don't be fooled
by the day; 'tis mountains in those waters, that make widows*.

Weaving through tall grass, we arrive at the Burns cottage.
A rose-covered trellis welcomes. Anna O'Malley lived 92 years;
34 longer than John Burns, her younger spouse—the boy next door.

John O'Malley's interest in Clare's immigrants shines as brightly
as that evening's full moon. As I walk back to the one Island Hotel
I shout *moove* to Irish cows who don't.

I leave grateful I descended from Clare Island, where women make
circumstance into opportunity, where unspoiled relatives live,
stubborn as the cows who wouldn't move.

The Kerrigans Carry On
Michael Joseph Kerrigan
9-6-1876, at rest 11-24-1942

Michael Joseph, a third son of eight born in County Sligo, Ireland. Some say let the bold go; others say the cautious were left behind. Michael, my grandfather immigrated to Boston where he married Katherine, a girl from back home. In 1910 Mike & Kate left Boston for Chicago. Mike found employment there as a city transit driver, bought one home after the other to shelter his growing family of six. A job, owning land—were not accessible to Ireland's working men. At age 52, my grandfather became a single parent; he had four children. After his wife died, he worked irregular hours and housed Irish immigrants. Awakened by their constant music, *Pat,* he said, *can you place a pillow under that fiddling foot of yours?* Marie, the oldest daughter, left high school to cook for borders and family. Jack, the oldest son took on full time employment, later dropping dead at work. Their father mourned nightly: *My son, my son.* James, my father, a high school basketball player, earned a college athletic scholarship. He couldn't be a student and a breadwinner, both; he couldn't accept the offer. *It's a poor family that can't afford one gentleman,* his father lamented. As an adult, Eileen, the youngest, searched for years for facts about her mother.

On the day the bombs blitzed Pearl Harbor, James scribbled a note to my mother on the inside cover of a matchbook: *You are my lucky strike.* The matchsticks remain unlit. They married in 1942. James, an officer, served in the Medical Corps, accompanying the sick and wounded back to their homes. He shared his birth date with William Butler Yeats. The Benbulben Mountains, topped year-round with braids of snow, stand guard over Yeats' resting place in Sligo, where I traveled to meet my father's cousins. They left home only to earn their educations at Ivies in the States, visiting the Chicago clan along the way back, returning to give their very best to Ireland. The Kerrigan home, a modest two-story farmhouse gabled to the road, remains in family hands in County Sligo. To stay or go has long been the dilemma.

Kate, from County Sligo

Katherine Tahaney Kerrigan
5-16-1883, at rest 7-27-1926

I never met her, my father's mother. Her one photo's in black & white. Records say that Kate, was the oldest of eight. The census ten years later reveals her Mother as dead. Kate gone. Did she blow a kiss or shout an expletive as she sailed off Ireland's coast? What better reason for an Irish lass to undertake a perilous voyage than for love? In Boston, Kate married Michael Joseph Kerrigan, my grandfather, five years her senior from Sligo.

Years later, I ask about Aunt Marie about her Mother: *My Mother's younger sister Agnes was sent passage. Agnes came to help with the younger ones after Kate lost, Elizabeth, in infancy. Jack and I got to go to the show twice a week. Mother loved nice things…*Aunt Marie writes what she watched as a child peeking from a stairwell: *With party cakes in the pantry, Saturdays were reserved for fun and dancing. Fiddle players rattled our house. Greenhorns danced jigs and reels in the basement where beer and liquor were brewed. With arms linked at the shoulders, making a circle, dancers whirled round and round until the ladies' feet rose off the ground.*

Kate died at 43, on an operating table with no one to hold her hand. James, my father, was 8. By then Kate would have known that little Seamus slept with a basketball, hid his pennies in his socks away from his older siblings. After her Mother died Marie left high school to cook for borders and the family. Dad, smirking like a young offender admits: *We shipped young, childless and out numbered Aunt Agnes back to Ireland crying and praying "Godhelpus" as if it were one word.*

Loss of a parent, occurring in youth, lingers like a meal you once tasted and still hunger for. Fifty years later, his blue eyes watering, Dad remembers his Mother: *a happy person with an infectious laugh, full of fun.*

Love Famine

Preparing Sunday dinner for one,
I grabbed a heart-shaped potato out of a sack,
Indentations on each side, as if it once had
major arteries and veins that connected it
to some living creature. Skin reddened, so thin
a fingernail scratch would leave a scar. Plump
at the top, narrower at the base, looking to have
had four proper chambers, but cold and hard.

I could not peel it, nor boil it, could not
mash it, let alone pierce it, after vowing
never to break a heart again. There are some
blows from which you don't recover.

Could this talisman be a reminder of Ireland's
Great Hunger: *an Gorta Mor?* When oppressors
forced farmers to return what they grew, when one
potato was a meal. Millions poisoned by a fungus.
Starved, died. Famine death pits across the country.
My ancestors left hungry, with empty pockets,
hearts breaking, never again to see hearth or kin.
Could their crossings for food, for freedom,
for work, also have been chosen for love?

Is this valentine, this potato, a caution
about a heart that beats on daily without care?
Or is it a good omen that my own love famine may end
before my hungry heart completes life's banquet?

Lucky Enough: Chicago, 1960

If you are lucky enough to be Irish
in America, story telling is in your bones.
you build tales about what you remember
and what you don't. Storytelling, not a side dish
rather an entree at any celebration.

If you are lucky enough to be Irish
you could sell an Eskimo a refrigerator,
but never teach an Italian how to cook. Without
those *Pisans* you & yours might endure
another Great Famine.

If you are lucky enough to be Irish
subverting the oppressor is an intricate marker
woven into your DNA. One Irish Catholic so
adept he charms a Chicago mayor and a few
Protestants to advance his campaign.

If you are lucky enough to be Irish
you commiserate with Jewish girls,
not easy to find in the neighborhood.
Learn Jews atone only once a year, while
Catholics go weekly to confess, confess, confess.

If you are lucky enough to be Irish
you call your friends *Dago, Wop, Pollack,
Mick*. You slap your neighbors on the back.
Although a few others are only concerned
that outsiders might move in,
might upend their home values.

If you are lucky enough to be Irish
you dream about dashing Latin lovers.
Any book entitled *Irish Erotic Art*
you know is full of blank pages.

If you are even luckier to be Irish
and female, you become linked
to women all over the world, who
like the Blessed Mother, think
their sons are God.

If you are lucky enough to be Irish, you are lucky enough.

Mothers in Mourning

Aran sweaters were originally knit
by Irish mothers, sisters, or wives
in unique weaves, specific to the county
from which fishermen sailed. The patterns
were later used to identify men
when their corpses washed ashore.
A suit of armor would have been lighter.
Many sailors refused to learn to swim
despite engaging in this dangerous livelihood
because *it only prolonged the agony*.

Do Chicago Mothers look through tears
for gang tattoos or identifying birth marks
on their sons lying on a slab in the morgue?
Mothers torture themselves, ask what hooked them,
longing to wrap them in their own shawls. Young,
black bodies piling up on the cracked cement alleys
or shot in public parks by gangs or police. Chicago,
I cannot forgive you for allowing so much carnage.
When did your streets become more lethal
than the Atlantic Ocean?

A Celtic Lament
Waterford, Ireland

You come to me in a dream
after many years gone, in Ireland,
womb for all my ancestors.
All day at the Waterford factory
I stand mesmerized, watching
bearded glass blowers, as flames
shoot from tubes twirling
in their mouths. Sand transformed
into hot, golden glass.
That night you crystallize in my sleep,
weary with a five o'clock shadow
to climb the stairs of the family home
I left so long ago.
You flow into my cupped arms,
where we recline nude on a four poster.
I hold you gently like wedding crystal.
My hands hum over your sharp edges.
Night leaves before you can splinter
my heart, etched with the pattern
of your comings, your goings.

Irish Summers

Ireland cries
a bit each day.
So many departed
broken-hearted.
Visitors pull up
their rain gear,
but she breathes in
her cool, clean air.
Drop, drop, drop.
Chats with herself.
Sniffle, sniffle, sniffle.
Gets over herself.
The sun peeks out
to make shadows
for this day's people.
Then she marches
into her long day
on the wrong side
of the bumpy road
knowing
crying feels good
when it's over.

Mo Cuishle: My Darling My Own,

an Irish term of endearment
Dad whispered on special occasions.

Mo Cuishle, you did us proud,
imagine the Queen's court
in the St. Patty's Day parade?

Such a strange whisper, it is remembered.
Such a sweet whisper, you memorize
the occasion on which it is spoken.

Mo Cuishle, are the church bells ringing
because you are getting married or
because you are on time?

We slowly processed down the church aisle
me holding the arm of one good man,
letting go for another.

We've a tiny Mo Cuishle,
when we brought his first grandchild home.
As soon as she could walk
she adorned her neck with his ties.

Unaccustomed to being
outside a sick bed
Dad visited with a gift of cologne.
Mo Cuishle,
Sorry, you needed this surgery.

My last Mo Cuishle.

Seismic Shifts

Sonnet During a Storm

Lights flicker inside, then outside; darkness claims.
Soon a thick white candle glows below
your pensive face in the sterling silver frame.
Over your chestnut hair, a bridal veil flows.

I will love you until the twelfth of never.
Water soaked snowflakes crack tree limbs in half.
I will love you until the hemispheres sever.
My love is stronger than Mother Nature's wrath.

There's a storm between us, as you try to find your way.
Behind the window's glass, circuits fire, sparks careen.
Words and winds blow by; neither of us are easily swayed.
In this cold, blue bedroom, only your beauty can be seen.

Singular child, your face, the last visage I see tonight.
Be it the last one that I will behold on my final night.

Getting Serious
James Kerrigan 6-13-1916, at rest 9-3-1978

The prospect of my father dying hovered over my girlhood. On Father's Day, our last, we started talking politics: *Women had a lot of class before this Equal Rights Amendment. But Nancy,* he said, *I want to get serious...I don't have much energy.* He moved on, *Nancy, never embarrass a man. Men do stupid things, pull them aside, tell them in private...*

I don't remember another soul in my home, or when the reality descended on me like a heavy, theatrical curtain, that I was listening to his closing monologue. Sitting on the floor near his feet, I was looking up. All I could think about was the father who sat next to me like another appendage for eight hours while my young husband underwent neurosurgery. He sat still and upright in a chair, his back to the fireplace, gazing over my head. The season was early summer, but felt like fall.

When I'm gone, if there are any problems, go to Uncle John.

This moment ended as most do in families—someone bursts in with another agenda. How much more could he have shared with me if we had more time? Dad was readmitted to a V.A. hospital for the last time. What unspoken thoughts, what fears wandered around the corridors of his brain as he lay there with hospital nurses changing the surgical dressing on his back? *Good job,* he whispered to them as he would to us; a soldier to the very end. Noticing he hadn't eaten, I offered his universal cure for what ailed us kids: a milkshake for a sore throat, an unfair grade, a lost fight. *It goes down so easily,* he commented as he accepted. Each time I exited his hospital room he'd say: *Now, you take care of your mother.*

In the end we agreed that Mother was *managing quite well,* but I would *do my part.* He danced in this last round with the grace of *Gentleman Jim,* as his father had called him. He yielded to the next generation with agility. *You kids will just have to figure it out.*

On our last day outside, I pushed him in his wheel chair around the grounds while we both sang *Blue Skies.* It was a day when no other song would do. How could I leave this man who looked both ways before I crossed any street?

Winter Solstice

Annamae Burns Kerrigan
11-10-15, at rest 12-25-2000

I listen to snow,
see the fireplace
embers' last glow.
My mind drifts
to an ancient burial
cave in Ireland
where sunlight shines
through darkness
for seventeen minutes
during the solstice.
It pierces into
the center of souls
where all colors meet,
connects us
to everyone
to ourselves.

On our final day
to see you,
be with you
without you
white roses,
white baskets
embrace the ends
of your casket.
The light put out
from your blue eyes;
the shortest day of our lives.
While we process
out of our church's
dimness,
that day's last light
and the gentlest,
downy snow
falls, whitening
our hair.

Bocelli & You

Ascend.
step by step
to the upper deck
at the Opera House.
Audience lined up like unread
library books on tall shelves. You
would have devoured every one of them.
Heights, I hate them, save for high notes that awaken.

Down
Bocelli's voice cascades.
My tears drop like whole notes
falling off the music's black lined page.
Eyes closed. I see you, with youthful brown hair,
your tears, a stream on your face, scrubbing on hands & knees.
The Metropolitan Opera bewildering, beckoning on the kitchen radio.

Applause
interrupts my reverie.
My mind resurrects you, Mother,
conducting the routine symphony of daily life.
Without you my focal point is gone. No one loved
sad arias like you. Loss, a theme recurring in any great love.
Your voice, taste, music is in me, sometimes we even hummed in tune.

White Space

Another door has clicked shut.

You believed the dying would speak of death,
    maybe not, who then to turn to?
The phone no longer rings on Sundays,
    you are alert for it anyway.
The mystery solved,
    you lay the book down gently.
You resolve to keep on dancing, keep singing,
    even though you can't now.
The last note of the tenor's aria drifts off
    the notes reverberate all day.
The curtain on a life is lowered,
    you hear soft applause and polite silence.
You cross out a friend's name in your address book,
    try to pen a tiny epitaph.

You leave white space for what you can't write.

Seismic Shifts

Pillars of my family, gone.
Flying alone to Chicago.
Security staff wave wands
as if blessing each passenger.
No one flying after 9-11.
Flight attendants huddled in the tail.
I hear everything.
I hear nothing;
terror without terrorists,
finally, the anesthesia of wine.
I know no one;
no one knows me.

Untethered in space,
seat belts no anchor, cabin dark,
heart knocking against my chest wall,
I see those New Yorkers in
free fall, free fall, free fall.
Solitude takes seat F, buckles up,
trench coat collar pulled up
to the cold of night, profile invisible.
Rationality, in a grey pinstripe suit
is behind me, muttering.
Faith is in the cockpit in uniform.
I know no one;
no one knows me.

In Chicago the next morning,
I throw off the covers of sleep
that allowed me to forget
in the peace of night
that death landed,
that there had been a seismic shift,
all of which I remember
by the time I grab my robe,
my overcoat of tears.

I Had A Dream

Not the Martin Luther King kind,
with freedom visible down
an ever-narrowing path, supporters
marching, marching.

In my dream I was looking at
the back of a naked man. His body
filmy, like black & white negatives.
The man had lost all his hair.

A fresh incision crawled down
this man's long neck, zipper like.
If it burst open I feared damage
to his brain, to his body.

A well-healed sickle scar, seared
on the upper right quadrant of his back.
Under it, a fist-sized open wound
oozing, oozing fluid.

On awakening I rubbed my eyes,
to realize my father's and husband's
bodies had melded together
in my dark dream of night.

At daybreak I saw two men
playing the cards they were dealt,
while I sat helpless to make
anyone better.

My dream, like *Les Miserables*,
where no one got what they wanted
but passion poured out
of every pore.

Homesick

I was never as homesick
as when sitting alone in a hotel bar in Newark
glued to a huge, flat screen TV to watch
the Chicago Cubs pitch and field
their way into the World Series.
Me, their only fan in the bar.
I would have given all I own,
to be standing in the crowd unable to move
in front of Wrigley Field at Addison & Clark.

In Chicago *Rainbow Ice Cream* might still be open.
Leaves might still be on the trees in October.
And no New England or West coast hot dog rivals
the steamed, mustard laden, tomato and
its secret spice I relished in Chicago.

Along with millions of Americans
I cheered on the Cubs, young athletes
dedicated to the notion that the whole
is greater than the sum of its parts. Somehow,
over what seemed to me a sliver of years
and too many Augusts where the Cubbies proved
they weren't ready for the big leagues—
I became an outsider,
me, the export who'd been traded.

Chicago's no longer the Second City.
In 2016, the Cubs won one for the ages.
Along with my joy, a strange melancholy
rose up in me. After only one glass of wine
it all came flooding back. All the coaches,
catchers, pitchers and players in my life—gone.
Even the umpires who called me out—dead.

There is no one left in Chicago to go home to.

Women's March on Washington
for Anna May O'Malley,
June 8, 1905, at rest January 10, 2002

On an eight-hour bus ride to the Capital,
I raise you up from the cold, cold earth.
You who walked or waited for buses all of your life.
You, who worked as a Chicago school teacher.
You, who would not protest if someone intentionally
stomped on your black laced mid heel shoes.

At the march, women use markers, crayons,
and paint to show their convictions on poster boards.

> *I will not go quietly back to the 1950s.*
> *Keep your rosaries off my ovaries.*

It would have shocked you. You who bought us
jelly-filled doughnuts if we biked
to a summer morning weekday Mass.

Among 600,000 marchers, we are moved by the crowd.
Bodies gridlocked like puzzle pieces without our soles
ever touching the ground—some chanting over and over

> *Women's rights are human rights.*
> *Equal pay for equal work.*

You would've prayed for our souls, not for an annual raise.

Anna May, you gave us free homework help
when we appeared on your doorstep without even
a phone call. We took the stairs two at a time
up to your three-room apartment with its paper-thin walls
that absorbed some of our young ignorance.

> *Librarians for Facts*

would have been your favorite sign, held high
by a gray-haired schoolmarm.

    Peace

one of your frequent greetings. If I protested
some perceived injustice, you would whisper,
while softly brushing my cheeks:
Let it go, luv. Let it go...
You who could let the worst go.

At Last This

The Field's Clock
Chicago, Illinois

In 1897 Marshall Field erected this,
once bronze, now turquoise filigreed clock
on the edge of his marble palace.
Its time displayed in Roman numerals,
for the many friends, couples and families
who would meet under it, or not, then leave
notes stuck on his store's plate glass windows.

This department store whose retail motto:
Give the lady what she wants, was the site
for our many brief encounters, where I ran
to meet you in three-inch spectator pumps,
hatless, bobbed hair blowing, clutch purse in hand,
my navy striped dress billowing like a spinnaker
in the gales of the *Windy City*.

You leaned under the suspended clock
of this *Beaux-Arts* building, one long leg bent
behind you on the building's limestone exterior,
bracing yourself for the routine wait
which you reported was *worth it*.
Sport coat slung over your shoulder,
shirt sleeves rolled up to feel the embrace.

Only the clock and I and the cornerstone survived;
Field's name gone the way of other partnership deals.
Years later, I stand on Washington & State streets,
thinking of you. I don't recall we ever missed each other,
and I know it's you I'm waiting for, to round
the corner today. I leave buoyed by the architecture
of a love that forces time to stand still.

Hand-Me-Downs

Layers of disappointment
keep the mothers warm,
a winter storm after years
of temperate weather.

My daughter throws a snowball
as we adore my granddaughters
gliding and shuffling around the rink,
shiny new ice skates gleaming.
*Your hand-me-downs,
that's all I had*, she murmurs.

Sadness follows me
all the way home.
Icicles hang from the gutter,
tears dangling in midstream,
frozen in time.
The house cries
to come in from the cold.
I'm ready to run out
to the sporting goods store, barefoot,
plaid flannel nightgown and all,
to buy new white figure skates
for a forty-year-old mother of two.

The account book of her childhood,
not fully funded. The payload
of parental guilt never overdrawn.

*The old skates weren't so bad, Mom.
My friends saw Nancy Kerrigan's
autograph inside them.*

Santa Gets it Right
for Anna Katherine

Finally, Santa got Superman's
gender correct. How you loved
your shimmering royal blue dress
and cape trimmed in red.
On the chest a big, gold & red *S*
set on a yellow triangle, as if
Superman had morphed into a feminist.
You stretched it out near your bed,
ready to be jumped into when called.

That entire magical day,
you flew through wrappings
as if they were clouds.
Your sister, *Super-baby*, fluttered
right behind you, her pink
blanket tucked like a cape
around the neck of her
red-footed pajamas.
You landed on both feet
arms raised like a prize fighter.

If I were Lois Lane writing
for the *Daily Planet*, I'd say
I'm delighted the world changed.
That you are already able
*to leap small buildings
in a single bound.*
With my x-ray vision
I see you super girls will soar
through life on imagination
and sheer will power.

Playground Dust-Up
for Nora Jane

Two boys follow
your blue, blue eyes
and blond hair
to three school swings.
All are airborne, legs pumping.
Some big, third grade girls shout,
Get off the swings, first graders!
Nobody moves.
Get off the swings, midgets!
The savvy boys take off
when the biggest girl
shakes down your swing.
You plant yourself
with feet that do not yet
reach the asphalt.
Not a muscle on your
six-year-old body moves,
not even your mouth.
You hear the *little voice*
in your brain say,
I'm not getting off.
You don't.
Your fourth-grade sister confesses,
I'd a been so out of there!
Mom demands *What happened?*
The recess bell rang.

You leave the kitchen
with a swagger and swish
to your pleated skirt,
one that wasn't evident
to us that morning at breakfast.

At Last This
Sea Bright, New Jersey

Our only child's summers
sizzled away at a community pool.
Evergreen Park's *Aqua*. My mind sees
her tall father in his life-guard chair.
My old back feels his young hand guide my dive.
Only heaven could drag him away from the sun.

She sat in a guard chair with his whistle
hanging well past her waist. Three aqua pools
now buried under dark earth—
for condos, for discount stores?

Relentless screams of kids
shouting Marco Polo from a pool
surrounded by sizzling cement. Stripping off
swimsuits in dressing rooms with nothing
but the sky for a ceiling, some days in the rain.
Not a single tree in sight for shade.
All we could give is what we had had.

This Chicagoan finds swimming in the Atlantic
like diving into a bad Margarita. My tanned daughter
stands next to my un-tanned self
on cool New Jersey sand as my granddaughters
and their friends streak by carrying
surf boards like notebooks.

Sounds of swooshing waves calm.
Salt water air sure tops the smell of chlorine.
A cabana to change in, dinner most nights
with their neighborhood friends,
an outdoor movie on the beach, a breeze.
She unites the years with ease—

That we all lived out our summers
in wet bathing suits is what counts.

Wellspring

If I see a cardinal
in the back yard
he is usually alone.
Bluebirds come in pairs.
Could that be how they
earned the moniker
birds of happiness?
Plumage brilliant
against brown grass.
Chirping, chirping,
dancing around each other
never stepping
on the other's toes.
Looking out my window
for absolutely nothing,
coffee mug in hand,
this morning they
become you and I,
in our early years,
pecking, flying
everywhere together,
me under your wing,
you insisting I could soar,
take off, build a nest.

And then the you I knew
was gone.

Decades later,
you are in my roots,
in the fiber of my being.
I've been more faithful
than I ever meant to be.

Aurora

Charles P. Jarasek
June 10, 1942, at rest July 27, 1999

I gave you the dawn
of my stormy life,
the fullness of my hair
the assuredness of my walk
the energy for the struggle
my singleness of purpose.
My laughing face.
It mirrored yours.
Yet you
did not live to say
you were aware
of this simple truth.
I lost too.
I lost you.

Beginning our love
in the daylight
of youth, a gift.
I find you anew
as I write.
Our love
not an illusion
written in sand.
This comes to me
in the evening
of my years.

Harvested

They paved paradise and put up a parking lot.
—Joni Mitchell

Drove by old Chicago haunts this fall, under plaid trees, cruised for my childhood one. The small starter homes raised, leveled, gone. Our Queen Anne, demolished. Cleared for a hospital parking lot. The playground, the tennis courts, jack-hammered. Streets our *Schwinns* snaked around, rearranged. Aqua, the community pool, empty and dry as a nightly martini. Vital organs of my youth, harvested. At the cemetery, each name inscribed in granite, triggered a flashback of that family's habitat, built by children of the Depression. WWII veterans visited the sick after work, ran raffles. Wives organized luncheons and fashion shows. Profits built schools and churches. Most stayed married for life, even non-Catholics. Some sacrificed to the point of silent resentment. They saved for retirement. Phones had classy exchanges: Prospect, Beachwood, Garden. If I dialed one now, no one would answer. Their offspring ran away to coastal states. Some surfed life's waves, opposed war, went to war, blended two families, a few lived in the city's elegant high-rise condos. Two-career couples shared housework, changed laws, demanded leave. Grandparents a plane ride away. Families united by emails. Bedtime stories read on *Skype*. Phones are now smarter than we are. Global disasters are mitigated by rock concerts; smaller crises still amenable to hot, hand-delivered casseroles. What's been lost as important as what's been gained. You can tear down streets in first tier suburbs, but you can't erase the blueprint for a meaningful life. Flew back home, never wanting to have left, never wanting to return.

Notes on the Poems

The Godfather: John C. Burns was the announcer and commentator of *Something About the Irish* and *The Golden Moments of Music*, which were Chicago-area radio shows. He also served as TV commentator for Chicago's annual St. Patrick's Day parade.

Dancing at Lughnasa: This play by Brian Friel is about the Ireland's Celtic harvest festival.

Eastern Adulterer: Chicago was christened the "Second City" by A.J. Liebling, who felt it was, culturally, second to New York City. In 1952 he published a book called *Chicago: The Second City*. The label stuck; it's generally used pejoratively.

Conversations on Clare Island: The island appears three miles off Clew Bay on the West coast of County Mayo, Ireland. 1700 people inhabited the island at the turn of the 19th century. Now it is home to 150 year-round residents.

"Too Ra Loo Ra Loo Ral" is an Irish-American lullaby composed by James Royce Shannon.

Mothers in Mourning: Out of 751 murders in Chicago in 2016, 500 were black men and boys.

Winter Solstice: Newgrange is Ireland's rebuilt prehistoric monument that predates the Egyptian pyramids and Stonehenge.

About the Author

Nancy Kerrigan's formative years were spent in Chicago. Later, she became a New England transplant. Coursework at Trinity College in Hartford initiated her path to writing poetry. She has attended Wesleyan University's Writers Week and workshops at the Frost Place in Franconia, New Hampshire. Finishing Line press published her chapbooks. *The Voices: The Poetry of Psychiatry* was published in 2009 and *High Heals & Sneakers* came out in 2015. Kerrigan spent two summers participating in Bay Path University's Creative Non-fiction Graduate Seminars on Dingle, Ireland, writing and giving readings of her work there. She has taught in the Schools of Nursing at Loyola University, St. Xavier University and Yale University. Her work in hospitals and in her own psychotherapy practice has contributed to her insights about individuals, children and families. Poetry, for her is the artistic medium of choice to portray human relatedness and the complexities of the mind.

Acknowledgments

I wish to express my appreciation to those who have published my poems previously.

"Behind Closed Doors," *Caduceus*: Vol. #8. Yale Medical Group at Art Place

"Billy Collins Goes to Nantucket," *Nantucket: A Collection*, White Fish Press

"Denouement," "The Field's Clock," *Everybody Says Hello*, Grayson Books

"Doors," "Eastern Adulterer," "Hope Is," "The Mack House," "Mama Drama," "Men Working," "The Rocker," *High Heels & Sneakers: My Balance Myth*, Finishing Linge Press

"The Field's Clock," "In the Cards," "Lollygagger of the First Waters," *Everybody Says Hello*, Grayson Books

"For the Women Who Ride Buses," *Kalliope: A Journal of Women's Literature and Art*, Florida Community College, 2007

"A Future in Past Tense," *Connecticut River Review*, 2017

"The Heart Shaped Space," *The Voices: The Poetry of Psychiatry*, Finishing Line Press

"The Night the Mannequins Moved," "Rude Awakening," "Sonnet During a Storm," "Your Own Vietnam," "Wellspring," *A Place for What Was*, Grayson Books

Thank you also to Barry Moore for permission to quote from his song lyrics.

"City of Chicago," Barry Moore IMRO

www.ingramcontent.com/pod-product-compliance
Lightning Source LLC
Chambersburg PA
CBHW052100070526
44584CB00017B/2272